The Animal Bridegroom

THE
ANIMAL BRIDEGROOM

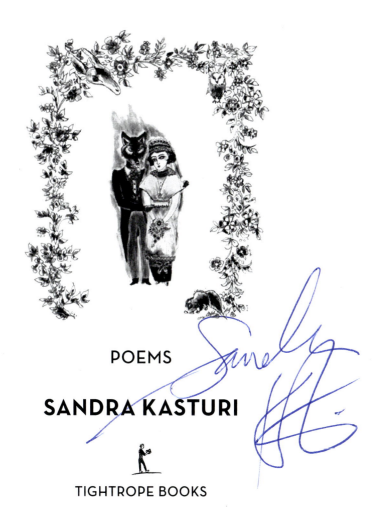

POEMS

SANDRA KASTURI

TIGHTROPE BOOKS

Copyright © Sandra Kasturi, 2007

ALL RIGHTS RESERVED. No part of this publication may be reproduced, stored in a retrieval system or transmitted, in any form or by any means, without prior permission of the publisher or, in the case of photocopying or other reprographic copying, a licence from Access Copyright, the Canadian Copyright Licensing Agency, www.access copyright.ca, info@accesscopyright.ca.

Tightrope Books
17 Greyton Crescent
Toronto, Ontario
Canada M6E 2G1
www.tightropebooks.com

EDITOR: Myna Wallin
COPY EDITOR: Myna Wallin
COVER ART: Kristi-ly Green
COVER DESIGN: David Bigham for Metal Ox Design
AUTHOR PHOTO: David Bigham
TYPESETTING: carleton wilson graphic design

Printed in Canada

  Canada Council   Conseil des Arts
for the Arts   du Canada

ONTARIO ARTS COUNCIL
CONSEIL DES ARTS DE L'ONTARIO

LIBRARY AND ARCHIVES CANADA CATALOGUING IN PUBLICATION

Kasturi, Sandra, 1966–
    The animal bridgegroom / Sandra Kasturi.

Poems.
ISBN 978-0-9738645-6-4

    1. Fantastic poetry, Canadian (English). 2. Feminist poetry, Canadian (English). I. Title.

PS8571.A8667A65 2007   C811'.54   C2007-900313-3

for all those who are,
or have been,
lost
but not forgotten:

Great-Uncle Julius
& Great-Aunt Toni

my father-in-law, Don

‡

never least,
for Brett

TABLE OF CONTENTS

9   A Brief Introduction—Neil Gaiman

INTO THE WOODS

13   The Burning Woman
14   Chaos Theory
18   The Gretel Papers
20   The Birch Tree
21   Verses for the Lost
22   Estonian Witches
24   Cadmus Reminisces
25   Sea Wrack
26   Spring Has Slipped Behind a Chair, Forgotten

LYING WITH WOLVES

31   Lying with Wolves
33   Five Cantos from the Prayer Book of Aphrodite
34   Carnaval Perpetuel
38   Faustus Tigris
40   The Stars as Seen from Alberta
44   Skinchanger
45   Berry Picking with Jane
47   Love with a Mermaid
48   The Left Love Department

SPELLS & ENCHANTMENTS

53 Things the Rose Tree Knows In Spring

55 A Daughter's a Daughter

57 Taken Root

58 The Fisherman's Wife Revisited

59 Joanne Ironing

62 The Changeling

64 Frankenstein's Monster's Wife's Therapist

65 The Swan Maiden's Tale

THE UNBINDING OF SPIRITS

71 I Speak for the Serpent

73 After Misreading Emerson

74 Merlin to Nimue

76 Seven Poems

77 Gaslight Elegy

80 The Flayed Woman

81 After the Flood

82 Old Men, Smoking

84 The Unbinding of Spirits

85 On Writing an Elegy for You, Whom I Have Lost

87 Falling

89 Notes

90 Acknowledgements

93 Author Bio

A Brief Introduction

People forget that myths have power. They forget that fairy tales are older than they are, and wiser, and have survived a great deal more than any people have to be with us today.

People forget that stories were crafted, long, long ago. They forget the deep wood, believing the forest to be far away, and not inside each of us.

People forget the joy of story as they grow older. They forget the joy of poetry, of finding the perfect word, of turning a phrase like a potter turning a pot on a wheel, and they believe, mistakenly, that poetry is not pleasure but work, or worse, something good for you but unpleasant-tasting, like cod-liver oil.

Sandra Kasturi has not forgotten any of these things.

Neil Gaiman

INTO THE WOODS

THE BURNING WOMAN

Listen!
You can hear her pale voice
from within the conflagration.
It always speaks truth.
It always lies.
She crackles like marrow-bone
when she walks.
Her eyes and mouth are open
and burn like magnesium.
She is a contrary Gorgon;
everything she looks at
is forced into frenzied life.
If you are very lucky
and can run after her
until she catches you,
you can put her in a canning jar
to hold in the air:

a blaze of fireflies
to light the darkness.

CHAOS THEORY

1.

The way through the forest
is walked by shapeshifters
and wolves who suffer from indigestion,
having eaten too many grandmothers.

You may find a coterie of little men
occasional princes
and some sleepy guy with the head of an ass.

At any given moment
the path may twitch
and
(you can only enter the forest
by exiting the forest).

If you leave a trail of breadcrumbs
they will only be eaten (with Camembert)
during the cocktail hour.

2.

The way through the forest
is danced by wild girls with sharp teeth
who throw streams of frantically beating butterflies
into the air.

There are hulder maidens with cow-tails
and twelve-headed troll kings
who peer slyly from their caves
and from between the trees.

If you ask them for directions
you will merely be deboned
like a chicken
and made into soup.

3.

The way through the forest
is always bargained for
(payment is in salt).

If you are ever asked to supper
by a Court of exquisitely fair beings
seat yourself
smile politely
remember not to eat or drink
anything and take your leave
as soon as possible.

4.

The way through the forest
is always a pattern
and forever random.

(You must look before you leap
You must look before you look.)

There are helpers in the forest:
giant caterpillars who smoke too much,
tin men,
delusional old crones
who aren't really old crones at all
trees that preen and mutter to themselves
in the wind.

5.

If you forsake the forest
it will follow you
surround you
permeate you
though you may not recognize it
(you can't see the forest for the trees
you can't see the trees for the forest).

6.

The way through the forest
is sometimes crossed suddenly
by the White Stag
who will give you your heart's desire
if you catch him.

Your heart's desire is to leave the forest.
No one ever catches the White Stag.

7.

There is no way through the forest.

THE GRETEL PAPERS

They phoned me yesterday
to tell me what you'd done to yourself
and all I can think
is why and why and why
I suppose I should have known
that it would lead to this
but in truth
I never saw it coming, Gretel
I never saw it coming

You were always gay and golden-haired
before those weeks in the woods
and even now
it's that image staying with me
not that of the silent young woman you became
the woman they tell me
is lying in a hospital bed
invaded by tubes

Did you put your head in an oven
to atone for what you did
what we did
in that little cottage
in the woods
all those years ago

Is this your way of shouting?
Your trail of breadcrumbs, Gretel?

We had no choice
but to try to survive

me with my chicken bone
through the bars
and you silent with fear
waiting for just one chance

I saw what you did to the old woman
Gretel, and only applauded your courage
your quick wit

Why you never said anything
to me of all people
over all these years
I who suffered with you
who stood fast beside you
after the breadcrumbs
and the way home
had disappeared

Gretel, my sister
I'm coming now
to take your hand again
push back the darkness
and lead you through the woods
once more

But remember
Gretel
remember my love for you
and know that when I sit by your hospital bed
and feel your fingers in mine,
know that I,
I will not be fooled
by a thin chicken bone

THE BIRCH TREE

The birch tree knows things the fox doesn't.
It knows stillness, its own sharp shadow.
It knows bursting greengold gifts
and the shiver of disrobing leaves.
The birch knows the spread-out patchwork
seen from the hill, the whip
and gust of rattling wind;
the close mysteries of the earth,
that rooting joy
that mulching pleasure.
What the birch tree doesn't know is me.
But I know the birch tree.

VERSES FOR THE LOST

As a child, you have been lost in the forest—
Or perhaps left in the forest, you cannot be sure—
Your shoes humbled in dirt, your strawberry dress
Pinched by spindleshank trees; no fewer

Than a thousand eyes gathering yellow
In the creeping dusk. Who searches for you,
Lost strawberry girl? Who is it that follows
Your vanishing footsteps, your fading echo?

At the end of the path, even grandmother's
House will bring no solace—she's always worn
A wolf suit on the inside—and the further
Stray girls go, the darker things may turn.

How vast the wood is, if lost you choose to be;
That unbiddable deep, that changeling greengold sea.

ESTONIAN WITCHES

Estonian witches ride on canister vacs
it's hard for them to straddle those upright Hoovers
and brooms are just too old-fashioned
although I suppose some cling to tradition

They have nice homes too
no damp caves
or glass hills that'll blind you on the ride home
and no sugardy-candy cottages in the Schwarzwald
like those hypoglycemic German witches live in
and that weird house on chicken legs
in the freezing cold forest
that old mortar-and-pestle-riding Russian witch is partial to
well you can just forget it
Estonian witches like comfort

Mind you it was different before the war
then all they did was sit around knitting spells
into fuzzy looking odd smelling witch-balls
to throw after a wayward daughter
when she ran off with some high-strung anemic prince
invariably falling off a bridge into the river
and getting turned into a water lily for her trouble
a lot of work for nothing really
since the prince always goes whinging
to some hoity-toity Finnish sorcerer
and gets the witch's daughter changed back
a little soggy to be sure
but he takes her to the palace with him anyway
and then how's a self-respecting witch to hold her head up

That's why nowadays Estonian witches own condos in Florida
and visit the old country every other summer
(they let their daughters keep the house in Toronto
where they can shack up with whomever they please
prince or not)
let's face it
it's a lot easier getting a witch license in a developed country

CADMUS REMINISCES

Dragon's teeth
sown in our backyard
produced such an inundation
of small, fat iguanas
that Mother and Father
had several suitcases made.

SEA WRACK

On a seldom-walked pebbly shore,
I once found you lying
where the mercurial sea had flung you,
skin pearly-pale as a cavedeep salamander,
bits of shell
entangled in your net of hair.

I remember I stood quite near you
just looking
while the coy tide advanced and retreated,
until I had to reach down
and brush your still cheek
with one finger,
only to have your eyes fly open,
your eyes,
green as the bright sun through deep water,
and as indifferent.

You lay there, watching me,
merely waiting for the sea to take you back;
I stood and walked away,
and while I never turned to look
I am sure your eyes snapped shut
before I was out of sight.

Later—I did search for you
on what may have been
that same stretch of pebbly shore,
though I never did find anything
but some dried kelp
a fragment of chalky shell
and three milk-white scales.

SPRING HAS SLIPPED BEHIND A CHAIR, FORGOTTEN

*"Spring seems to have been omitted this year, and will probably finally
turn up in July where it will turn out to have been put under some
newspapers, or to have slipped behind a chair, and been forgotten
about."*

—Neil Gaiman

Spring has slipped behind a chair, forgotten,
as glass slippers years after the ball might be
(cracked and cobwebby and left in the corner),
or the unused spinning wheel, the peek-a-boo
coffin, the long-decayed donkeyskin.

Spring lies rumpled, beneath a newspaper
or in an unused room, squeezed out
as midwinter tales rush headlong
into golden-haired summer,
feverish with the business of living,
of happy-ever-after and marriages
to princes and huntsmen and transformed beasts.

How easy to slip off spring! that unfashionable frock
draped and left to fall behind a chair—
how simple to overlook that gustery wind
with its kites and kestrels,
the shy peeping of tulips
and the newfound promise of open windows:

Being taken to mad tea parties,
flung into the sky at the end of a kite-tail,
gone up faerie hills and maypoles,
down bursting, spell-breaking
rivers, onto the backs of butterflies
and constellations, to the underworld
and out again, dragging Hades'
astonished girlfriend into the open air
amid a gust of hawthorn blossoms,
chattering lilies and Easter hats
sprung fresh from the ground.

Let fall the fervid, heavy robes of summer,
those days fat with ever-afters and over-sweet
honeysuckle—they come too soon.
Turn back the sundial, re-bud the branches,
and let us dust off spring, pick it up
from behind the chair and shake it out,
linger in its cool folds, its clean embrace,
and let all other seasons await their blessed turn.

LYING WITH WOLVES

LYING WITH WOLVES

for R.

A woman who loves a wolf
can never be satisfied by anyone else.
All other creatures will disappear
from her heart.
The caress of a man or a woman,
a butterfly or a bear
will leave her dull, unburnished.
But a wolf's length of tongue
between her legs alone
is enough to change the new world order.
Ah, she will sigh, *ah, ah, ah.*

He teaches her music,
for wolves know music
better than they know almost anything else;
she drifts on the notes of his moonlit baying.
She gives him her words
(she has always had too many words)
preserved in canning jars by her grandmother,
now resting heavy in her woven basket;
he swallows them delicately each morning from her spoon.

A woman who loves a wolf
needs him beside her
inside her
his belly pressed against her back,
his teeth sharp against her shoulder blade.
Ah, she cries, *ah, ah, ah.*

Nights she sleeps in a curl
against his hairy body,
her red mouth dreaming,
the soft breath from his muzzle
chuffing against her pale neck.

She strokes
the thick brush of his tail
and buries her face
in the ruff of his throat.
He lays his head upon her,
his prickly whiskers moving over her naked breasts.
Ah, ah, ah.

The love of a lonely wolf,
full of secrets and strange midnights—
drawn out of the darkness
from hills thick with black oaks
valleys riddled with riddles—
that love is sharper than a bed of thistles;
each kiss pares away flesh.

The love of a wolf
can eat you up all the better.

Five Cantos from the Prayer Book of Aphrodite

Love is a black beetle,
chitinous, serrated,
many-segmented and complex.

Love is the soft ear
of a wild cherry flower,
a Japanese pen and ink.

Love is a strange sea bird,
fractious in its cries
as it flies inland.

Love is a chambered nautilus shell
thrown into startled hands
by a devilish sea.

Love is the fickle moon's round reflection
caught in a sieve
by the fishers of memory.

CARNAVAL PERPETUEL

1. BEFORE

The paths that lead to the ball are many:
they are often lined with the forgotten ashes of scullery maids
who have gone on to better things than picking lentils out of
    the hearth.
While wanting a ball is not wanting a prince
the two seem to go hand in hand,
a kind of logarithmic function of desire and fulfillment.
And so, scullery maid or princess,
we, each and every one, arrive at the ball
bedecked in feathers and fury.

2. MASQUE

We are given only two hands to use in the dance,
one always caught in the clutch of another,
and the second hand ticking
gently in front of the eyes:
spread fingers creating spyholes of flesh.
Had the fairy godmother thought to give the gift
of a third hand, instead of, say,
shoes never worn enough to be worth the price,
think how different the story might have been.

3. MIDNIGHT

Herr Drosselmeier, godfather,
maker of timepieces
and other ticky-toys,
we stand and bow to you.
You always knew,
in the way that godfathers know such things,
that the Prince is always the hardest nut to crack,
no matter how many hands are given to the task.
As for you, Carabosse,
keeper of clocks,
when did you leave us
to this solitary pirouette on the head of a spindle,
a waltz of one hundred years,
feet twitching like Father's eldest hunting hound,
fingers burning into straw, into gold:
we were the gifts given,
gaily wrapped packages in reversible paper
readied for this one or that one.
(You always said
twelve strokes weren't really enough
but what prince ever believed that?)

4. EVER AFTER

Beyond the glass coffin
beyond the glass hill
beyond the glass slipper:
only you and I,
a shadowy duet of parsimony and elegance.
How the creeping sundial does sweep us!
despite raggedy clothes, shoe-loss
and devious step-parents,
into the arms
of a tidy, anticipated future.
And there we dance, covered
in feathers and furbelows, bells and bobbles,
our hands given, as foreordained
to an endless parade
of velvet knickerbockered golden-crowned youths,
the unfolding of an infinite paper princeling chain.

5. THE END

Time is the mother of invention
and the sister of theft.
It is the glass globe of hand-spun conjurings
on the end of the spindle-shaft,
dancing in the shadow of the long hand,
twirling in the lee of the short hand.
Here, each dance has the fractal precision of chaos,
whether prince or prisoner, scullery maid or princess,
each part contains the pattern of the whole:
wish and desire
and eventually
(if you wish)
(if you desire)
(if you dare)
even love.

FAUSTUS TIGRIS

Amber is the soul of the tiger turned to stone.

—Chinese saying

The tigers on hot fur pads
ink their way
across quilted sheets of parchment
and collapse sprawling on my
                    bed sometimes
                    just sometimes

their coppery hides
wound with black ribbons of words
the air peppery with their
EXHALATIONS! of red
meat-jungle-rain-yellow breath

stalking
my remotely human face
tails whisking
stories from my palms
pawing, clawing,
finding my unkempt heart
my stripy soul

until I
am left dumb
nothing but a
            wordless
            crackling
            tiger

pawning my hot fur soul
leaving an amber paperweight
for the devil's desk

THE STARS AS SEEN FROM ALBERTA

You, naked at the foot of the bed,
arrange yourself into Greek statue poses
for my benefit

I have hair all over my body
you said over the phone
good
I said

You parade around naked
showing me your hairy body
your animal presence
I lie in bed and watch
hoping you'll suddenly be overcome by desire
and pounce on me
that's why I'm wearing the silk dressing gown
The woolly socks may not be sexy
but it's colder than I thought it would be
here in Banff

You come back from the bathroom
and dive under the covers
spoon me
you say
so I do
my cheek pressed against your hairy back
my arms around your waist
pulling you tight against me
I think of places on your body
I can lay
my hands
(readiness is all)
but I think you're falling asleep
and won't really notice

You're going to break my heart
I said once
You looked at me
You're so sure of that?

yes

I said

These few mornings together
and you always get up two hours early
before you actually have to leave the house
I notice you need all this time
to dance around the living room
or lie in bed and channel surf
and read the daily paper
from beginning to end
strictly in order
but there was this one time
you let me have the crossword and the comics
even though you hadn't got to that section yet

the privilege
I say
and don't you forget it
you say

I orbit you
in this state of continual bemusement
it's the way you eat bananas
without using your hands
it's your tatty terrycloth bathrobe
it's when you don't shave
and I want you to rub your scratchy face
all over my body
it's the compulsive way you read the paper
and yes
it's you posing as a Greek statue
in Banff

Just before I fly home
your musician friend with the nice hands
says to me slyly
so what do you call each other
any special names
affectionate terms—
anything
erotic?
you and I look at each other sideways
mmm, not really
we mumble

but you called me by my name, once
it's true
I remember it
you lying in bed looking at me
saying I am beautiful
saying *Iloveyou*
not on the phone
but in person
saying my name
it almost stopped my heart
I am telling you

it almost stopped my heart

SKINCHANGER

for Patricia A. McKillip

after you had searched my head
for ancestral knowledge of shapeshifting
you took me out onto the plain
and taught me
the shifter's dance
and after three long nights
under a clear May moon
I learned the *change*

you scored my palms
with the shape of horns
my hands running blood
but it was worth it
oh
worth it
to run hooved
like lightning
across the savannah

all bone and

    hair and

      blood

        pumping

          in   the   w   i   n   d

BERRY PICKING WITH JANE

I'm berry picking with Jane
in the wavery alien heat of July,
wading through the thick molasses forest
and mosquito deerfly air
of a northern Ontario summer.
Time trails behind us in fat gusts,
eddying around scratched ankles,
only to catch and snarl in bramble-bushes.
Nothing else is in motion
but the occasional slow slide of a salty droplet
that begins its travel from the nape of the neck
and eventually wends its tortuous way
over water-rich flesh
to settle gently in the small
of the back, that plumping curve.

We pick the plump blackberries
Jane and I, with our soft city-girl fingers
sneaking one berry
and now another
into our mouths,
knowing that one on the tongue
is worth two in the bush.
The colour stains our fingers
lips and tongues
as deep and lush a burgundy
red as antique velvet,
Sangre de Toro.

Then Jane finds a clearing in the wood
and something mangled
lying near the centre
that isn't a racoon.

Can you smell it asks Jane
Can you
Can you smell it
There's no other scent like it in the world
Once you've encountered it
You'll never mistake it for anything else

Afterward, we retrace our wake
through the heated air
and tangled berry-laden bushes,
to the open twilight of summer evening.
A fire has been raised on the stony shore of Georgian Bay,
flickering waves of heat toward us—
two dirty would-be peasant girls with their covered baskets.

We found something dead in the wood, I say.
Their heads turn
and I realize they must see
the stains darkening around our mouths,
shadowing our hands.
It's from the berries I'm about to say,
but then I see Jane out of the corner of my eye
licking her fingers and smiling that sly smile of hers.
And I decide to say nothing
nothing at all.

Love with a Mermaid

I have often wondered:

the scales on my bed
butterfly tri-coloured
better ice cream
than I've eaten in years
coral reefs
of epic proportions
and salt residue
in the bathtub
the mussel shells
on the floor
my hair full of sand
from the pillowcase
webbed fingerprints
waterlogged on the door-latch
and my copies
of *Moby Dick* and *Captains Courageous*
left slightly damp and half read

But I never knew love to make much sense

THE LEFT LOVE DEPARTMENT

for Jason & Jennifer

One day a man on a train to Vienna left his love behind. He had carried it with him on his travels through Europe before, but this time he absentmindedly put the love in the overhead compartment and completely forgot it. When the conductor came by, he simply sighed and put the left love on his cart, along with the other lost items: the usual umbrellas and handkerchiefs, a handbag or two, an elderly and overweight pug dog, half a sandwich, and no less than fourteen maps and eight Berlitz guides. The pug dog ate the sandwich and then promptly fell asleep on top of the love, squashing it rather badly.

It might have turned out differently if the man hadn't lost his love on a Friday. But he did, and the usually conscientious conductor's cart was shoved into the corner by the train station's weekend staff, who felt it certainly wasn't their responsibility to finish up work left by anyone else. Then the cleaning lady had a go when she moved the cart to get at some cobwebs. With the pug dog having set off on his own adventures long since, the love slipped off the top and fell onto the floor, whereupon the cleaning lady got part of it stuck to the bottom of her shoe. The love was dragged all the way home with her and only came unstuck on her uneven front walkway, where it remained until the milkman tripped on one of the paving stones the next day. He fell face first right into the love and was so covered in it that when the cleaning lady opened the door and went to help the milkman up, his face purely shone. The left love struck her full force, and they were married inside of six months.

The man who had left his love on the train was travelling back from Vienna soon after and stopped at that same station. He asked if there was a Left Love Department, but no one seemed to know what he was talking about. He went home very sadly and wondered how he was going to explain it all to his wife.

But that good woman took one look at him and knew instantly that he must have accidentally left his love somewhere while travelling. She smiled and took him by the hand down to the root cellar. And there on the shelves, shining in the dim light, row upon row, were hundreds of glass canning jars, each filled to the brim with love; the man's wife had carefully preserved what they had to spare each year, to set by a store in case of emergencies. She opened a sealed jar, and they stood there together, breathing in the heady spice of love, while several miles away, the elderly pug dog stood confused at the railway crossroads, the irresistible aroma of love coming equally from two different directions, so that he could not make up his mind which to follow.

SPELLS & ENCHANTMENTS

THINGS THE ROSE TREE KNOWS IN SPRING

for Helen & Dan

The rose tree knows little of love.
It dreams, as all flowering creatures dream,
of things it does know:
wind, the small rain and falling thunderstorm.
The speaking of magpies,
the scurries of round, brown mice.

The rose tree knows even the step
and rattle of postmen,
the hollow bark
of the neighbours' dog
and the shivering
of too-early lilies in their nearby beds.

The rose tree dreams, not of love,
but of openings: one bud, then others,
each a scarlet kiss,
a burst of future—
planting's promise,
the marriage of elements.

The rose tree remembers
and dreams of its storybook counterparts,
thick and thorny and secretive,
growing over paths and princesses;
and of its wild brethren,
small and hardy, hiding
from the hot summer tar
of roads and ways,
and the places roads lead to.

The rose tree dreams of roofs and walls
(so close!) and the two lives ticking inside,
clocks sped up by joy, by joining—
shoes together in the cupboard
or running up the curling staircase,
two pillows, mingled books and songs,
new basil slanting on the window ledge,
artemisia downy-soft in the garden.

The rose tree now remembers
the sun's coming fierceness and the gift
of manmade rain from a pierced tin can,
of hands that peat and mulch and prune together.
Hands that till and turn the earth,
grow roses, trees, turn house to home.

What the rose tree knows and dreams is true.
It now knows love, as loved things do.

A Daughter's a Daughter

A son is a son till he takes him a wife,
A daughter's a daughter for the rest of your life.

—Traditional

Persephone lies
eyes open, smiling
a heavy coin under her tongue
waiting for her bridegroom.

Demeter cries
above-ground, a common harridan
screeching for her mislaid daughter
while the land lies fallow
the people starve
and Hades, unblinking, smirks.

In the grey palace of the dead
on the floor of some bedchamber
he places his bone-cold hand
against her belly
and she
surfeited with the seed
of the pomegranate
smiles
and does not hear
winter crackling on the surface.

Demeter spies
her daughter
under the cold ground
and drags her by her hair
unwilling
into the open air.

Persephone tries
to escape her mother's wary eye
each and every year
to return to her handsome and remote bridegroom
while Demeter wishes wholeheartedly
that she had given birth to a boy.

Taken Root

Stranger than fiction
my daughter
grows in the garden
I can just see her
outside my window
there, behind the tomato plants
she dips and sways
larger every day;
it is all very peculiar
I could have sworn I planted dahlias.

THE FISHERMAN'S WIFE REVISITED

I caught you in the sea like a flounder
and when I had worked the hook out of your mouth
you said you could only give me one wish
so I cast you back in and caught you twice more.

JOANNE IRONING

Joanne is far gone into the Eastern provinces
with their strange tides
and whipping winds
where the sands creep into her house
and the sly beach grasses stray across her threshold
when she isn't looking.

Away from the smell and steam of her ironing board
it seems only the wind straightens her skirts now,
her iron just a small rusted weight
in a forgotten corner.

She calls me,
from a conch shell pressed to her ear,
and I can remember her ironing:

I sat on her sofa then,
half asleep in a cup of chamomile
watching her raised hands
twirl her flowered skirt
set it flying through the air
a dance of muslin and peonies
finally settling into an elegant drape
over the back of a chair.

Such small living room magics, Joanne
that you have long surpassed
now that you have been lured and lulled
by the smell of salt
and the hush of sand.
I hear the sound of the sea in your voice
across these many miles where I sit
by the avocado tree you grew yourself
and your rampant potted ivy
that I am slowly killing.
But between these gifts
I have managed to keep some of you,
some of you in my house.

When you take in the tide
do you think of me; I've stopped
ironing here in the city
far from wind and wit
and water, trying to knit
my own spells.

If I find my way to you
from my house in this desert—
perhaps I can leave behind my iron,
my machines, my cigarettes.

It would be easier to find you
without the brightness of the city
but I can almost see you from here.
Joanne, you have straightened

into a blond willow
an ash
a beech
your quick agile fingers dream
sepia photographs
that you send me:
marble monuments,
textured grasses and sharp-relief bluffs
by the Eastern coast,
each in its way another breadcrumb
leading to your doorstep.

THE CHANGELING

My great sta ey-eyed goggle-child
lying heavily in its basket on the floor by the fire
watching me as I move about the room
its sucking wet fish mouth
opening
closing
a monstrous baby bird
as my shadow passes over it
doing nothing but eating me
out of house and home
house and home

Finally I ask the grey-haired witch-possible
of a neighbour lady
what's to be done
and she tells me sure enough
so I am boiling water in the two eggshell halves
over the fire
the not-baby-thing watching me
when it starts to laugh and laugh
and says its stupid rhyme
just like the witch-wife promised

Though old I be
As forest tree
Boiling water
In an eggshell
Never did I see

Then these elves or goblins or pixie-whatsits
that just make the toe of your boot itch
come scurrying in and before you can say Jack
Robinson

They leave me my human child
and carry off their changeling in turn
funny thing though
this baby just gapes and gawps and eats and drinks too
and I can't seem to remember
and my witch-neighbour won't tell me
when the original exchange took place

FRANKENSTEIN'S MONSTER'S WIFE'S THERAPIST

She tells me she's happy now.
They've reconciled. He spends
most evenings at home
and they've started to try
to make babies: he bringing
their limbs home, she
with her size 10 sewing needle.

The Swan Maiden's Tale

You used to be a bird.
Well, once upon a time.

But this is what happened,
what will happen, what is
happening:

One day you strip off the cape
and the shape
on the grassy bank of this pond you swim in
and dive into the water as a girl.

Life's an endless holiday for you and your bird-girl friends
but sometimes it catches you out
while you're submerged.

It happens sooner than you expect, in fact.
The others get away while you're underwater
so it ends up being your feather cape he finds.

But it's okay because he's a prince
who says he finds you *bewitching*
or something equally original.
Oh.
You say.
Or something just as clever.

You never get used
to this business of hanging
out with royalty.

Smug as anything
he carries you
naked
to his castle
and has you
washed and waxed
clothed and groomed
primped and perfumed
until you're good for nothing
but wedding and bedding.

Being rescued isn't all it's cracked up to be
but it's sort of fun for a while.
Then you just get bored.
After all, how much embroidery can any
bird-girl take?

So you wink and wheedle,
ever the tease, ever the sly-boots,
anything
for that cloak of feathers.
Or you sigh and sob—
ever the martyr, ever the madonna.
You even promise
to stay with him
until the end of time
or some such fluff,
if he lets you have one last flutter.

But he just smiles
and looks confused
as if your words are a small child's—
misunderstood, but still treasured.

Or sometimes he frowns,
as if you're speaking
a foreign language.
And maybe you are.

In the end, though,
you have to tell yourself,
enough's enough.
You search each room yourself,
stone by stone
from turrets to dungeons.

But for all that work—
the spying,
the sighs, the simpers—
you still don't know
where your featherskin's hidden.
You never would have thought
he was that clever.
For all his misconceptions,
you're still there, aren't you?
Always a bird-girl, never a bird.

So no more flurries of melodrama.
And no more needlepoint.
In fact, you don't do much
of anything anymore, do you.
You simply fake
contentedness.
For the sake of the baby,
you like to think,
but really, for your own sake.
It's a lot easier that way,
don't you agree?

As for him,
he's kinder than ever now.
He does everything, simply
everything for you
You just snap
your fingers.

And it's only
in the late hours of the night
when you lie
awake
and have to listen
to his heavy breathing beside you
with the baby fluttering and fretting in her cradle
that you begin to wonder
where the plucked feathers
of your soft new bed
have come from.

THE UNBINDING
OF SPIRITS

I Speak for the Serpent

If I speak for the serpent, the serpent
may speak for the bird.

—Robert Bringhurst, from "The Calling"

I'm an old woman, grown round from swallowing imaginary birds
In their blurred trajectories, their complicated algorithms.

The soft down of erne and grackle, the sharp speed
Of the European bee-eater, the rhythm of starlings.

It's always best to eat impossible things in the morning:
Birds. Infinity. Square eggs, love.

I diminish, recede into the distance. A diet of irrational figures
Sits uneasily on plate and palate.

Things spill upward, flutter in my throat,
New voices: whir and peck. Whir and peck.

I've become too rough and frantic, too infantile.
Losing years of wisdom with each beat of wings, heart, head.

Perhaps I will trade for an old voice, heard
At the beginning, lost or stolen, out of earshot now.

I could learn to squeeze myself into wiliness and low cunning,
A new-patterned frock. I could speak to and for the serpent.

An agony of misappropriation. Still:
Smooth silence, geometric eternity.

I would grow large again, swallowing my own tail.
But I'm fast from whirring, sharp from pecking.

Maybe the serpent should speak for me.
And I should speak for no one.

AFTER MISREADING EMERSON

Why should we import rags and relics into the new hour?

—Emerson

How many rages and relics
do I import into each new hour
wandering from my bed in the mornings
my head on fire, my hands
clenched with lightning
ready to pour myself into a teapot
to rant and roar and roil

How many madwomen
have I been keeping in the attic
bundling bodies
into decrepit steamer trunks
mildewy with travel
and ripe with cat piss
looking for a baseball bat
to bang up and down the stairs
in a Jack Nicholson *Shining* fury
I'm not gonna hurt ya
I'm just gonna bash yer fuckin head in

There is no sense
in my ranting and roaring
my rages and relics
the light was already dying when I got here
the madwomen long gone
the teapots dusty
and no bats within easy reach

MERLIN TO NIMUE

I have almost made it through the long winter without you
although the nuts that you grudgingly doled out to me
in the late autumn, one by one,
like you, are now long since gone,
having been gnawed by me in the close darkness
of your enchanted oak tree.

I have been curled up inside this tree
for quite some time, my fingers woven into the darkness,
or perhaps worrying at that one
sharp piece of nutshell that I am sure you
deliberately left behind for me
to discover after you had already gone.

All my magics are now completely gone,
faded away in the gloom of your hollow tree,
my brittle skin infiltrated by the creeping darkness
and by that whetted shell: a two-edged gift from you
(and somehow the only one
that still manages to pierce me

despite all efforts by me
to remove it). Now the tree
crackles with the winter wind and when the darkness
within echoes the darkness without, I can sense you
nearby, but on waking I know you are gone
and I am once again the only one

left here in this hollow space, from one
raw stretch of time to the next. As for the tree,
I sometimes believe it tries to nurture me,
but it is only half alive, and I am already too far gone,
bound to this small ensorcelled place by you,
lulled and lullabied by winter and darkness.

You did warn me that this darkness
would be all that was left to me
as I dreamed the centuries away in my tree,
all light leeched from me and gone
the way of my long-vanished nuts, but for that one
sharp shell lodged in my heart, that is you.

Though you are gone, I did almost make it through winter
        without you
but the icy darkness has finally bound me
and a prison for one is my hollow tree.

SEVEN POEMS

These are my poems:

One was found thrown high into the branches of a tree.
Another I dug up at the site of a crumbled vicarage.
The third and fourth I have been keeping
        in Ziploc bags in the freezer
        to preserve their freshness.

The fifth poem was baked with blackbirds in a pie.
Number six rests in a cork-stoppered green glass jar
        in my aunt's kitchen,
        next to the brass chickadee bottle opener.

The last poem is orbiting earth in a golden casket
        occasionally disturbing news broadcasts.

GASLIGHT ELEGY

The breath of the past,
that flickering image—lost
in the glare of modernism and electricity—
the muslin rustle of Victorians
trailing feathers and fans,
dark paper silhouettes,
lace cut-outs of doilies and teacups,
that glimmer in gaslight, in memory,
then catch, burn,
disappear into ash,
itself the ghost of fire.

Gaslight haunts the electric
until that current must remain ever bright,
stamping out shadow and mystery,
chasing away the spectres of James and Jacobs.
Electricity never sleeps,
knowing a careless moment, a second's lost vigilance—
and gaslight will once again creep
over the pointed rooftops,
steal into the waiting, verdigrised lampposts,
through every faded living room,
sighing past Baker Street and Whitechapel,
comforting as a long-forgotten London peasouper.

How forgiving is gaslight!
How fond of the collective imaginations
of humanity!—its reluctant parent,
giving birth centuries ago.
Never quite forgetting,
gaslight relives its past life
in smoke and mirrors, old films—
games of cat and mouse with
Charles Boyer and Ingrid Bergman.

Gaslight whispers to us of hidden attics,
furniture that moves by itself,
and forbidding steamer trunks
filled with jewel-sewn opera gowns,
crumbling statues and idols of Astarte,
rocking chairs hag-ridden by the late Mrs. Bates,
and even pieces of the True Cross
kept inside the moth-eaten stockings
that fill several dresser drawers.

Gaslight is tricksy,
kind and maternal;
will suggest, hint and hide,
reveal and repel.
It will remember all
and forget everything.
Gaslight is a girl's, a ghost's,
a governess's best friend.

And whatever ghosts may walk and dream
by gaslight, they are haunted themselves
by a future too bright and rational
for planchette and table-rapping,
by tales told not by glorious idiots
but by scientists,
full of terrible reason.
Until they, or you, or I
will fade evermore swiftly
leaving no mark—
just a soft, nearly-asked question,
or a wish recanted,
an ethereal knock on a door,
which, when finally answered,
reveals—
a ghost
of a ghost
of nothing.

THE FLAYED WOMAN

One late Monday afternoon
when she had been home for an hour
she took her sharpest Ginsu knife
and
starting with her fingers
removed her entire skin
stretched it out
and thumbtacked it
to the floor
Now
each morning she stands
and dances
dances a red muscle-driven dance
around her skin

At night she arranges herself into a tight ball under the bed
and lets the skin answer the door

After the Flood

There are beasts in the towns
that have tumbled in a deluge from humans;
they have fallen from our sleeves
and even now peep out of our ears

I myself once had an antelope spring full grown
from a crack in my skull
and gallop away into the late morning

Several people have left camels on buses
and businessmen keep stirring up
crocodiles in their briefcases
or perhaps it's alligators;
they are never really sure until they are eaten

It has become increasingly tiresome
to discover sparrows by the thousands flying out of one's porridge
and African Pygmy Hedgehogs scrabbling in the bathtub
of course nearly everyone has had cows by now

We cannot seem to purge ourselves
of this inundation of large and small creatures
while there are fewer and fewer people on the streets

I even saw a leopard driving a Volkswagen the other day
and the television will show nothing but "Wild Kingdom"

I don't know where the humans have gone
but I think there are still a few in the city;
they peer doelike from between curtains
and never answer the door.

OLD MEN, SMOKING

You can see them standing singly or in clusters on street corners
Or sitting, calm as toads, in quaint but seedy coffee bars,

These old men who smoke and don't speak English.
They stare into the distance, seeing the drowning

Of the Titanic, the Lusitania, some obscure Estonian ferry,
Experiencing the wash of history. It leaves them clean,

Weathered, their eyes turned that strangest of blues by the sea,
The wind, the turning of years. These old men who smoke

And don't speak English—they know all the secrets of the
        universe,
Revealed to them in each glowing ember that flies away

From their mouths into the world. These old men—descendants
Of Prometheus, who, having stolen fire, passed it down through
        the ages

To old men who never grow older or die. They are immune
To cancer, to weather, to the voices of women. They simply smoke,

Cast embers into air, into history, mutter in foreign tongues
No matter what country they are in. These men with their gnarled

Gardeners' hands never really smile, never really see you,
But you know them, know them from past incarnations,

From memory, from myth. Maybe they do smile, inwardly, secretly,
At our mad scurryings and busy bodies. Such guileless crocodiles!—

Sitting, steadying the tilting world; smoking, obscuring the truths
We cannot bear to know; humming in the voices of God.

THE UNBINDING OF SPIRITS

What frail spectres can we begin to conceive
out of darkened bedrooms and glass-blown pride?
Conjuring tongues and gin-chilled fingers relieve
us of our private hauntings, turn them inside
out upon the carpet. Can we not inspire
peace—not this hag-ridden, ghost-hackled perturb
of an existence? Give one thought to what dire
sorrows may come forth, what we may disturb?
Yet here is grief. I have been waylaid.
I am gone to frantic clutching, a raving
of words, braiding together things unsaid,
things imagined. Mourning's bright weaving.
From my drowning bed, dragged by tides' rebound,
my spectral words, pulled to depths where they unsound.

ON WRITING AN ELEGY FOR YOU, WHOM I HAVE LOST

Tell me how we do sit and brace—
shore ourselves up by any means:
the backs of chairs, the edges
of tables, your sister's arm,
your father's shoulder, pillows
for the bent spine.

Old letters, sandbags,
that ugly sweater
you so love,
comfort books thumbed
through for decades,
propped under your fevered head,
keeping company with your wrist,
itself sprained under the weight of anguish.

These winter days will freeze you upright
as much as press you low
near the feet of uncounted ghosts
who will themselves bend,
and with hard invisible
fingers, roll you gently forward.
Gently forward.

What else can you do? Stand and stop.
Stand and stop with your weight
on a carafe of wine.
Two carafes, three. The smoke
from tobacco or burning photographs
will starch your shirt, straighten
you right up. Grief
and good writing
are all about carriage, stance.

A better mattress is needed. A bed
that does not list so, a firmer pillow.
Stretch the leg muscles,
strengthen the abdominal wall—
all these things will help you stand.
Perhaps a stronger, longer pen, too. One
that will reach from your hand to the ground,
for ease of leaning. A deeper inkwell.
A blacker ink.

FALLING

Let us now praise the falling things that fall
from trees and skies and gaseous nebulas,
things that succumb to the gravitational
influences of great and tremulous

bodies—winds or planets, rampaging gods—
things that drop like guillotine's falling calm,
or frenzied whirl of helicopter seed pods
from oaks so distant they blot out even the warm

of shooting stars. Let us praise the falling
of night, of winter, of the raining rain,
the hailmary high drop of ships' squalling
plunge down a wave-frenzied, storm-lathered plain.

Let fall empires. Let fall time's arrows.
Let fall ignorance. And wisdom. And sparrows.

NOTES

The quotation used as an epigraph for "Spring Has Slipped Behind a Chair, Forgotten" is from Neil Gaiman's on-line journal entry of April 16, 2002.

The line "wanting a ball is not wanting a prince" used in "Carnaval Perpetuel" is from Stephen Sondheim's musical, *Into the Woods*.

"The Left Love Department" was written for Jason Taniguchi and Jennifer Judge on the occasion of their wedding day, March 19, 2005.

"Things the Rose Tree Knows in Spring" was written for Helen Waters and Dan Lee, on the occasion of their wedding day, May 13, 2005.

"Frankenstein's Monster's Wife's Therapist" was nominated for a Rhysling Award in 2006.

"Old Men, Smoking" was the First Prize winner in *ARC Poetry Magazine's* 10th Annual Poem of the Year Contest, 2005.

"Verses for the Lost," "The Unbinding of Spirits," and "Falling" were originally written for my "Sonnet a Week" project, begun in February 2006.

ACKNOWLEDGEMENTS

I am tremendously grateful to the assistance provided by the Toronto Arts Council for this project. Many thanks also to *ARC Poetry Magazine* and to Mildred Tremblay for choosing "Old Men, Smoking."

Special thanks to the members of the Algonquin Square Table poetry workshop for their many years of input and coming to afternoon teas.

Thank you to kristi-ly green for her artwork and for understanding about the forests (and the lederhosen).

Many, many thanks to Phyllis Gotlieb, for the endless support, and for my first professional sale in *TransVersions*.

To the amazing Neil Gaiman—I don't even have the words.

And to dear Mr. Bradbury!—whose kind letters and voice mail have meant the world to me.

And finally, my overwhelming gratitude to Halli Villegas and Tightrope Books, and to my editor, Myna Wallin, for taking me on and whipping this collection into shape. I am awestruck by their hard work and commitment, and humbled by their friendship and kindness.

Some of the poems in this collection were previously published (some in alternate versions) in: *2001: A Science Fiction Poetry Anthology, Acta Victoriana, The Algonquin Square Table Anthology, The Annex Echo, ARC Poetry Magazine, Bloody Muse, Carnaval Perpetuel, ChiZine, Contemporary Verse 2, Daughter of Dangerous Dames, The Day I Ate Jupiter (and other poems), Grammateion, The Hart House Review, Latchkey.net, Lost Ages Chronicle, On Spec, Pursuits & Conjurings; Horrors, Guises, Rough Beasts, The Rhysling Award Anthology, Snow Monkey, Star*Line, Strange Horizons, Tesseracts⁵, Tesseracts⁹, Tesseracts 10, TransVersions, Twilight Tales, The U.C. Review*, and the World Fantasy Convention 2001 Programme Book CD-ROM.

AUTHOR BIO

Sandra Kasturi is a poet, writer and editor. Born in Estonia to an Estonian mother and Sri Lankan father, she is a U.S. citizen living in Canada. Sandra is currently working on an animated children's TV series, a novel and another poetry collection. In 2005 she won *ARC* magazine's annual Poem of the Year Award for her poem "Old Men, Smoking." She has also received several Toronto Arts Council grants, a Rhysling Award nomination, the Lydia Langstaff Memorial Prize for Writing, and a Bram Stoker Award for her editorial work at the on-line magazine, *ChiZine*. Sandra has written three poetry chapbooks and has edited the poetry anthology, *The Stars As Seen from this Particular Angle of Night*. Her work has appeared in various magazines and anthologies, including *Prairie Fire*, *On Spec*, many of the *Tesseracts* series, *2001: A Science Fiction Poetry Anthology*, and *Northern Frights 4*. Her cultural essay, "Divine Secrets of the Yaga Sisterhood" appeared in the anthology *Girls Who Bite Back: Witches, Slayers, Mutants and Freaks*. Sandra is a founding member of the Algonquin Square Table poetry workshop and runs her own imprint, Kelp Queen Press, which recently launched a new line of flimsies called "Loonie Dreadfuls." Sandra enjoys single-malt scotch, Veronica Mars and red lipstick. *The Animal Bridegroom* is her first book.